THE
GOLF
SWING
EXPOSED

Hands, brain, balance and Ben Hogan's last clues

**Back
BEACH**

STEVE MATTHEWS

www.thegolfswingexposed.com

First published 2013 by **Back Beach**
An imprint of Essential Media Pty Ltd
www.backbeach.net

Author Online
www.thegolfswingexposed.com

Cover image by Brad Hunt, Rhythm Films
Cover and internal design by Patricia McCallum
Illustrated by Patricia McCallum
Edited by Diane Furness
Typeset by Patricia McCallum
Printed in the United States of America by Lightning Source Inc.

National Library of Australia Cataloguing-in-Publication entry

Author:	Matthews, Steve, author.
Title:	The golf swing exposed : hands, brain, balance and Ben Hogan's last clues / Steve Matthews.
ISBN:	9780987341600 (paperback)
Notes:	Includes index.
Subjects:	Swing (Golf)
	Swing (Golf)--Technique.
	Golf--Technique.
Dewey Number:	796.3523

Contents

CHAPTER 4

CLUES FROM THE MASTER – BEN HOGAN'S SWING

CHAPTER 5

FIRST AID FOR YOUR SWING

Acknowledgements

There are several people whose talent and enthusiasm have made this book possible.

The golfer featured in the photographs: Christopher Dean plays out of the Murwillumbah Golf Club in Australia, where he shot a course record 66. He was the Tri District Champion in 2010 and was the low amateur at the Western Massachusetts Open when competing in the United States in 2011. Christopher is currently studying for a Psychology Degree with a Sport Major and is playing golf when university commitments allow.

The photographer: Brad Hunt of Rhythm Films has wide television experience, especially in live sports. He was the 2nd unit camera operator on Steven Spielberg's television drama *Terra Nova*. Brad captured Christopher's swing beautifully.

The book designer: Patricia McCallum has a passion for designing non-fiction books that engage the reader. Her flair and skill were invaluable.

The copy editor: Diane Furness has worked in publishing and education. She has a love of language and enjoys working with authors to create the best possible publication. She saw the early flaws and her suggestions always contributed to clarity and simplicity.

The copyright and image researcher: Brigid Baker guided us through the complicated world of permissions. And after searching far and wide, her dogged persistence paid off when she found the last known photos taken of Ben Hogan's swing.

The readers: Neil Jameson, Sandra Bernhardt, Steve Chapman and Charles Stewart were generous with their time and expertise.

A special thank you to the Murwillumbah Golf Club for permission to shoot on one of the most picturesque courses in the country. And many thanks to every PGA player mentioned in the book and to golfers everywhere.

Images
• Chris Carey: page 22 • Historic Golf Photos/The Ron Watts Collection © 2009-2019: pages 73, 75, 77, 81 • © Meng Yongmin/Xinhua Press/Corbis: page 65 • Sensory homunculus Image ID: 041490 © The Natural History Museum, London: page 18

Text
• *Australian Senior Golfer* http://australianseniorgolfer.com.au/396/ben-cren-shaws-simple-putting-tips: page 68 • from *Five Lessons The Modern Fundamentals of Golf — A Golf Digest Classics Book*, Ben Hogan (with Herbert Warren Wind), published by Golf Digest/Tennis, Inc. 1985: pages 22, 30, 31, 47, 74, 76, 79, 84 • NEW OXFORD AMERICAN DICTIONARY ONLINE (2010) Definition of 'timing'. By permission of Oxford University Press, USA: page 56 • from *The Lessons I've Learned*, Sam Snead with Don Wade, published by Macmillan Publishing Company, New York, 1989: page 39 • Copyright © 1997 Condé Nast. All rights reserved. Originally published in *Golf Digest*. Reprinted by permission: pages 75, 76.

Every effort has been made to trace and acknowledge copyright material. Contact the publisher at www.backbeach.net to enable any errors or omissions to be rectified in subsequent editions.

About the author

Steve Matthews worked in television for 35 years as a news and current affairs journalist, program producer and writer. His long list of credits includes sports, documentaries, lifestyle programs and website production. He was also a writer on the first series of *MythBusters* for the Discovery channel.

While Executive Producer of *Sports Sunday* for the Nine Network Australia, he managed to promote his other great passion when he created and produced *The Golf Show*.

Steve is an accredited Community Golf Coach under a program run by Golf Australia. Currently he is coaching several players who are hoping to qualify for The Special Olympics golf team.

Towards simplicity

A perfectly struck golf shot is a wondrous thing. Watching a small white ball fly towards the target and land where you intended is a fantastic thrill. But for the vast majority of golfers, it doesn't happen very often. Only a fortunate few seem to know the swing code. The challenge for the rest of us is trying to decipher it.

Complexity is the main danger. It's easy to get lost in the details, especially the technical aspects. I was looking for a different route, one that was easier to follow. Beyond all the noise, I thought there had to be a simpler way to discover what lies at the heart of the action.

To see what makes the swing work, I took the journalist's approach: observation and research. Then, by active experiment, put it to the test. The first step was to identify the swing's critical elements, the essential drivers. By stripping the swing down to its bare bones, I could expose the swing's basic choreography, its body language. How do the great players move? What aspects of the body in motion do they commonly display? And how do they do it?

Ben Hogan's pure and powerful swing is still a major source of inspiration for many players. His ever-popular book of instruction was first published in 1957, but nearly 30 years later, he added something new. In the foreword to a 1985 edition, he revealed his own secret. It was a method that saved his swing and his professional career. What he had to say is well worth another look because it holds vital clues. The Ben Hogan chapter puts those insights into perspective. It also includes the rare photos taken at his last recorded swing demonstration. The pictures of his timeless swing, alongside his canny advice, go right to the core of the matter.

This book sets out to show you how the swing works and why it works best when your brain and body are in harmony. Armed with this knowledge you can start to build your own consistent action. And when your swing goes wrong, you will know why and how to fix it.

To Sharon for her patience, persistence and professionalism. Thanks Shaz.

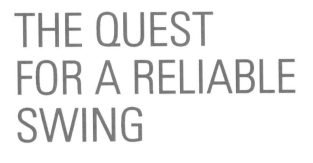

CHAPTER 1

THE QUEST FOR A RELIABLE SWING

A day to remember

In late 1997, I was with a television crew at the Twin Waters Golf Club in Queensland to cover the final of a Pro-Am team event called the Holden Scramble. Every year this long established contest attracts thousands of amateurs from clubs all over Australia. The teams that make it to the final round are joined by a player from the PGA Tour. This year there was a real buzz of anticipation around the course because the competition's host, Greg Norman, was in the mix.

For more than 25 years Greg Norman was one of the biggest stars in world golf. He was the first PGA Tour player to earn more than 10 million dollars. He held the number one ranking for a remarkable 331 weeks. Internationally he claimed more than 85 victories, including the British Open twice.

Norman flew in by helicopter and landed on the nearby practice ground. Just the day before, he had lost the 1997 Australian Open in a sudden death playoff to Britain's Lee Westwood. But if he was disappointed it didn't show. As always he was enthusiastic and ready to play golf.

The Scramble is an Ambrose or best-shot format and the Shark's role was to move through the field and play a tee-shot for each team. By the time they reached the long par 3 17th, the wind was up and causing all sorts of problems for the amateurs. At 202 meters (220 yards) and with a tight pin position, it was a tough hole even for a professional. But despite the tricky conditions, some of Norman's shots landed close to the pin and one almost dropped for a hole in one.

Greg Norman in full flight is a great show. For a tall man, his balance and posture are superb. All the way to the top, his backswing is long and fluid. His hands and arms draw the club back very slowly and deliberately. Then his brilliant footwork sets off a typically aggressive and confident downswing. Those lucky enough to be there that day witnessed an exhibition of superior ball striking.

I remembered watching Greg Norman when I came across some new swing clues in a magazine tribute to Ben Hogan. The article included a selection of Hogan's swing pointers. Some of these tips were new to me and seemed quite astonishing. His canny advice about how the swing works changed my own perspective dramatically. It was then I realised that although Hogan and Norman have distinctly different styles, they have something vital in common — *their hands and feet* appear to control the swing. They use their hands to set the backswing pathway and they use their feet to initiate the downswing.

Inside the ropes

I was Executive Producer of *Sports Sunday* in a decade when golf was experiencing rapid growth around the world. Club memberships were in demand and the public fairways were full of passionate golfers. I knew the network chief was a golfer and aware of the game's booming popularity. So I pitched an idea and he gave the go-ahead for *The Golf Show*. It was a half hour magazine program made by a small production team that by the end of its long run had broadcast 110 episodes. The show featured players and courses from home and overseas but the swing was the thing.

The Golf Show also came with invitations and when work commitments allowed I had the opportunity to play alongside professionals in Pro-Ams. Watching the best from inside the ropes is a great place to be and they were generous with advice. If I wanted more detailed scrutiny of the swing, the show's video catalogue was ideal. It included a collection of past and present champions — players like Peter Thomson, Jack Nicklaus, Steve Elkington and Nick Price, to name just a few among many.

The amount of golf available on the Internet was also expanding at an exponential rate. Today the swings of Adam Scott, Tiger Woods, Rory McIlroy, Martin Kaymer and the rest of the PGA Tour are accessible to every golfer and can be studied at length.

Armed with this wealth of material, my digging began in earnest. Ben Hogan once said that all the best players have major elements in common. If I wanted to understand the whole action, I had to find them.

Ecstasy and agony

Professional players make the swing look easy because they know how to make it work time and time again. So why, after more than 500 years of golf history, are so many of us still baffled by the action? My swing could fall apart at any time and I never knew why, let alone how to fix it.

An experience that has stuck with me for years, illustrates how fickle my swing could be. It happened one afternoon during a regular practice session at the local driving range.

I collected a bucket of balls, picked a spot and went through my usual warm-up routine. Then with a five iron in hand, I aimed at the 150-meter target — and right out of the blue hit a great shot. The ball came off the clubface with a crack and flew straight at the target. 'Fluke,' I thought and hit another one, with the same result.

Something to aim for —
everything working together
to deliver a well-timed
flowing action

From then on, every shot with every club was near perfect. The swing felt effortless and the timing was precise. My ball striking was so good that other golfers stopped to watch. Finally it looked like all the hard work was paying off. I couldn't wait to get onto the golf course the next day to put the fantastic new swing to the test.

What a miserable experience that turned out to be! Shots were either sliced or hooked and the ball landed anywhere but on the fairway. I had found a way to fashion every bad shot in the book and nothing I tried could fix it. So where was yesterday's swing? How could it vanish in less than 24 hours?

In the following days I tried to recall my swing but I couldn't get the whole picture in focus. How and why it had all come together so easily was a mystery. The only impression that lingered was a feeling of total harmony — mind and body working together to create a powerful flowing motion. I wanted to experience that sensation again.

Information overload

To find out why my beautiful swing had disappeared, I went looking for straight answers and workable solutions. They were difficult to find. Explanations varied widely; nothing was simple. Some descriptions of the swing were confusing; others were long and complicated. Books with titles that suggested an easy methodology often ran to more than 500 pages.

The truth seemed to be hiding under layers of complexity. There was no way of telling what mattered and what didn't. I was loaded with too much information, lost in a blizzard of swing thoughts and going nowhere. I was at a level of frustration and annoyance that was blocking my ability to understand the problem. It seemed like there was no way out.

Scientists who study how humans learn call this predicament Cognitive Load Theory. Their research shows that the brain can't retain multiple bits of information if it's arriving all at once. There's not enough mental capacity to deal with the front-end overload.

To demonstrate how golfers in particular are afflicted by too much information, American neuroscientists selected two groups of players from opposite ends of the ability spectrum — professionals and high-handicap amateurs. The experiment set out to compare the amount of activity in the region of the brain where motor skills are planned and executed. The results for each of the two groups were as stark as their skill levels.

As the professionals set up over the ball, their minds were fairly calm. They were mainly thinking about the shape of the shot and where to land the ball. Meanwhile, the brains of the high-handicap players were lit up like

The swing from start to finish takes about two seconds. During the final phase the club head is travelling at well over 160 kilometers per hour (100 miles per hour). There's no time to think, let alone change your mind, once the downswing is underway.

Christmas trees. They were frantically trying to remember all the things they should and shouldn't do. And they hadn't even begun to swing the club.

When presented with too much detail we get confused and can't remember the important bits. We become anxious and less able to make effective decisions. The outcome is known as analysis paralysis.

However, if our short-term or working memory is allowed to digest new information in easy chunks, one bite at a time, we are able to absorb, process and acquire skills faster. Information moves to our long-term memory with familiarity or practice. For instance, once we are familiar with driving a car, there is no need to think about every aspect of the process.

Myths and misconceptions

Trying to work with complex instructions and vague theories took me down plenty of blind alleys. Finding the way out meant busting the popular myths and misconceptions that regularly lead to confusion. In the following chapters we'll deal with some of the key ones, such as the illusion of weight shift and the false concept of centrifugal force. But before we move on, the biggest myth to debunk is head movement.

MYTH   DON'T MOVE YOUR HEAD

One of the game's oldest and ultimately flawed observations is 'You moved your head'. The call is typically made in response to a bad shot. But this core golfing belief is not necessarily true. Slow motion videos prove that many of the world's best golfers move their heads and they still manage to hit the ball proficiently. For example, Robert Allenby and Annika Sörenstam rotate their heads towards the target early in the downswing, in time with their shoulder turn, yet both players are excellent ball strikers.

Study any of the top players and you will find plenty of head movement, usually downward. Search the Internet for good quality videos of some of the best past and present players such as Ben Hogan and Tiger Woods. Play the videos in slow motion and pay particular attention to what happens to each player's head.

Videos of Hogan and Woods clearly show that both golfers lower their heads as they take the club back. They lower their heads even more as they bring the club into the downswing. And quite often it's not a little drop either. Depending on how much drive off the ground they require, their heads move a long way off the original starting position they established at address. Yet despite lowering their heads, they still manage to make excellent ball contact.

There are players, such as Louis Oosthuizen, who do keep their heads fairly steady and level. But it's not compulsory. The head is quite heavy; it's almost impossible to hold it absolutely still during the golf swing. However, beware of lifting your head — the sign of a faulty swing is a head that rises.

Head movement while putting is an entirely different story. If a player's head moves on the forward part of the stroke, even on short putts, the ball is likely to miss the hole.

A new look at an old dilemma

The golf swing is a relatively simple action. But it has been described and over-analysed to the point where it's difficult to see the big picture. Concerns like the angle of the spine, the ratio of hip-to-shoulder turn, or whether the arms are forming triangles tend to distract from understanding the whole swing in motion.

The swing is not a random assembly of moving parts; our entire body is involved in creating a unified movement. A less painful route is to forget the extraneous details and focus instead on what drives the motion.

Swinging a golf club is a lot like learning to dance. When dancers are familiar with the steps, they stop worrying about their feet and just go with the rhythm and tempo of the music. To develop a swing that works consistently you only need to learn a few basic moves — the rest is practice.

Clear heads and calm minds

You often hear tournament winners credit a calm state of mind for bringing them home successfully. Professionals are very aware that a cluttered mind is the perfect partner for a dubious swing. One of the main aims of this book is to show you how to stop the internal chatter and get to that calmer mental space.

Keep it simple is the key

In 1991 we took *The Golf Show* to The Royal Adelaide Golf Club in South Australia to cover preparations for the Asahi Glass Four Tours World Championship.

The teams were from Europe, Japan, Australasia and the United States. Among the Americans was Tom Purtzer, the man voted by his peers to have the best swing on the PGA Tour. It was a rare visit 'down under' and I was keen to see him in action. We caught up with Tom on the driving range and my lasting impression was of a swing that had no frills. It was easy, powerful and beautiful to watch. He happily shared his swing philosophy and the overriding message was to keep it simple.

Finding simplicity means wading through complexity and the investigation led me to some unexpected places. Neuroscience, the study of the brain and how it functions, and biomechanics, the physics of the body in motion, provided intriguing insights. Such scientific evidence does not get the attention it deserves. But for any golfer struggling to build a reliable swing, this knowledge is indispensible.

Exposing the essential drivers

The good news is that the swing does not have to be overly manipulated — the backswing and downswing are reflexive, part of our instinctive body choreography. Your brain, hands and feet are the essential drivers of the swing. They are the major elements that control the action, the team that harmonize balance and acceleration.

The hand–brain connection

One of my biggest breakthroughs happened late one night during a long editing session. While watching some of the world's best golfers in action, I realised that all the professionals shared something in common — their backswings were ruled by how they used their hands. To prove the point I went to the archives for a video of Ben Hogan. It was clear that Hogan was also using his hands to control and guide his backswing. The movement of the hands was unmistakable and seemed to be at the very heart of the action.

It was then I understood the power and influence of the hand–brain connection. Golf instruction is generally unaware of this primitive human link and that's unfortunate because your brain thinks your hands are huge. Neuroscientists have found that the motor cortex allocates more capacity to the hands than to any other part of the body. The motor cortex is where all voluntary muscle activity is planned and executed. Consequently the act of swinging a golf club can be defined as a direct conversation between your brain and your hands.

The partnership between hand and brain dominates all physical activity. It's on show every day in an endless round of ordinary yet complex skills like buttoning a shirt or using a knife and fork. The progress of human civilization is measured by what the hands can achieve, but we go about our lives oblivious to their fine motor skills and amazing dexterity. The hand–brain connection is instinctive and relevant to all struggling golfers.

Penfield's model of the Three-Dimensional Sensory Homunculus, The Natural History Museum, London. If our bodies developed to reflect the way the brain distributes power and control, humans would look like the model above — dominated by a huge mouth, large tongue and massive hands.

Since your hands are the tools that enable your brain to perform most of its best work, it should be no surprise that your hands play a major role in the golf swing. The communication between your brain and hands is so dominant that the rest of your body has little choice but to react, at all times, to what your hands are doing.

Hands lead the backswing

Allow your hands to lead the backswing and everything else takes its place in the sequence smoothly and reliably. There is no need to consciously control hip movement or shoulder turn — your body will automatically respond to what your hands are doing. This is great news for golfers who don't feel confident making a backswing, because trusting your hands to guide the way eliminates indecision and guesswork. The role of your hands in the backswing is explained in chapter 2.

In the backswing, your hands determine the path of the club and everything else follows their lead.

Hands in the downswing

Your hands are the fastest moving parts of your body; nothing can match them for speed. In the downswing, hand speed translates into club-head speed, and that means distance and hopefully accuracy for all your shots. The role of your hands in the downswing is explained in chapter 3.

Notice how far the hands have travelled in relation to the rest of the body. The hands deliver acceleration of the club head.

Hands, feet and balance

Your hands play a major part in balancing and coordinating your body during the swing. Throughout the movement your hands are in constant communication with your brain and your inner-ear balance mechanism to keep you upright and stable. If you are unsteady as the downswing begins, you won't be able to hit the ball long and true. Your feet and legs are the other active partners that safeguard your balance. As your hands and arms lead the backswing, your lower limbs anchor your body's movement. How to develop a well-balanced swing is explained in chapters 2 and 3.

try this: Start walking with both arms held against your sides. Then relax them in mid-stride. Immediately your arms will swing to counterbalance the leg on the opposite side. There is no need to consciously do anything; it all happens naturally. This simple test demonstrates how your brain, hands and feet automatically coordinate your whole body to keep it in balance. Their work is fundamental for human stability.

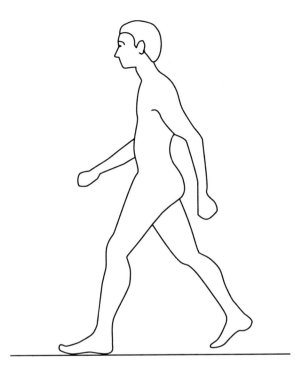

Balance in action

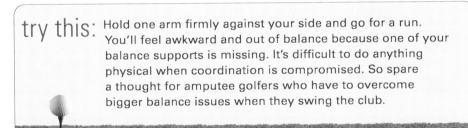

try this: Hold one arm firmly against your side and go for a run. You'll feel awkward and out of balance because one of your balance supports is missing. It's difficult to do anything physical when coordination is compromised. So spare a thought for amputee golfers who have to overcome bigger balance issues when they swing the club.

The role of the hands in maintaining dynamic balance is plain to see in sports that demand big body movements like football, gymnastics and surfing. But their influence is also evident in gentler pursuits such as snooker and darts where the hands are called on to make smaller but well-defined actions.

Whatever the physical activity, the feet and legs carry out equally subtle work. A darts player needs stability just as much as a footballer or surfer. Their sports may be poles apart but the brain's demand for good balance is a dominant factor. Success in any sport depends on it.

Kelly Slater, winner of multiple world surfing championships. Note how he is using his hands to keep his moving body in balance and under control. Great athletes in any sport make everything they do look graceful and effortless. Dancers call it 'having good hands'. It's no surprise that Slater is also a very capable golfer.

The kinetic chain

All first-class players have the ability to generate energy in the backswing and the skill to deliver a decisive downswing. Their powerful and fluid swings are the result of basic physics in action. Ben Hogan acknowledged the science of the swing in the 1950s when he said it was like 'a chain action in physics'.

A body in motion produces kinetic energy. The word *kinetic* comes from Greek and means 'to move'. As your body moves during the golf swing, kinetic energy is transferred from one part of your body to the next. Science describes this movement as a sequential rotation or kinetic chain.

The power of the swing is generated when you move through the backswing. Energy is not produced by the downswing — its function is to let the stored energy out.

Building energy via the kinetic chain begins at the start of the takeaway, as soon as the hands move the club into the backswing. To create an efficient and fluid movement, your bone and muscle connections have to move in a well-ordered motion. If you get the backswing started correctly and let your hands show the way, every link in the backswing chain will do its job as intended. The function of the downswing is then simply to release the potential energy. And it happens in reverse order — feet first, hands last. The energy is released from the ground up just as Greg Norman demonstrated so clearly at the Scramble.

Generating energy — the ground reaction force

The ground reaction force (GRF) enables you to create, hold and then discharge the energy of the swing.

The GRF is explained by Sir Isaac Newton's Third Law of Motion: for every action there is an equal and opposite reaction. It's always in play between the ground and your feet whether you are running, playing tennis or swinging a golf club. All of us use it quite naturally when we are walking. Any sport that makes contact with the ground exploits the GRF.

During the backswing, the GRF is generated through your feet and legs. As your hands and arms turn your upper body around, your feet push down, the earth pushes back and the GRF intensifies. Your feet and legs act as a solid brace to hold the backswing energy in place. Then your right foot gives the signal to start the downswing by pushing away from the ground.

Push off to get going. Sprinters use the ground and their feet to explode out of the blocks and accelerate away. Releasing the force as rapidly as possible translates to faster running.

Surprisingly, very little golf instruction emphasizes or even mentions the GRF. There are sports that teach elite athletes how to use it; baseball academies in particular put a lot of emphasis on how the GRF drives the action for batters, pitchers and fielders. The lack of emphasis on the GRF in golf instruction is an example of how we ignore crucial information because so much of our focus is on the details. It's like worrying about all the parts that power an automobile when the only thing the driver has to do is grab the wheel and step on the accelerator.

To appreciate how fundamental the GRF is to all physical activity, imagine being suspended in a harness above the ground. Your ability to move, let alone swing an arm downwards with any kind of force, is severely limited. It would be barely possible to hammer a nail into a bar of soap. How to use the GRF in the backswing and the downswing is explained in chapters 2 and 3.

Releasing energy — the passive dynamic transfer

The function of the downswing is to release the energy generated in the back-swing efficiently and effectively. It can be achieved through a release technique I call 'the passive dynamic transfer'.

The word 'passive' applies to your hips and shoulders. Keeping them in a relaxed attitude allows your arms to move smoothly and rapidly in the downswing. 'Dynamic' refers to the forces, initiated by your feet and legs, that promote the free-flowing 'transfer' of energy from one side of your body to the other. This technique is precisely how the professionals are able to use their arms efficiently to achieve optimum club-head speed.

A relaxed body attitude gives your arms and hands plenty of room to swing the club through the ball at top speed. Any tension held in your hips or shoulders impedes the ability of your arms and hands to swing the club freely.

This phase of the downswing is also known as 'clearing the right side' or 'getting the hips out of the way'. But these terms don't clearly explain where this phase fits in the kinetic chain. How the passive dynamic transfer works to deliver a consistent and powerful downswing is explained in chapter 3.

Timing your swing

The passive dynamic transfer holds the key to timing — that moment when everything moves into place so that your hands and club can make precise contact with the ball. The best swingers of the club are able to hit the ball consistently because their technique delivers good timing.

One of the best ways to see the truth of the swing is careful observation of the best players. But right away you'll see that all their swings are different, especially their backswings. How they take the club back appears to be irrelevant to the outcome. Making a solid backswing is important, but the part that matters is how and *when* players make contact with the ball.

All the best golfers share one vital characteristic — at impact their positions are virtually identical. They achieve good timing by releasing their hands at the wrists *at just the right moment* so that the club can accelerate through the ball.

You probably remember those exceptional moments when the ball flew off the clubface with absolute ease and you wondered, 'How did I do that?' But if you don't know how you did it your chances of repeating it are slim. That's what happened to me all those years ago at the driving range. I had discovered the secret of timing without knowing why or how to reproduce it. The art of timing is explained in chapter 3.

The way ahead

To build a good swing you only need to grasp a few essentials. Understanding how to manage your hands and feet is the key to creating a swing that doesn't go missing in action.

Your *hands* matter because they dominate the conversation with your brain regarding movement and balance. They initiate the backswing and everything else follows their lead. It's simple to do and delivers a worry-free backswing every time.

Your *feet* matter because, working together with your hands, they keep your body in balance. The feet also generate the GRF during the backswing and they alone initiate the downswing. The pay-off comes when you learn how to co-ordinate your hands and feet throughout the swing.

The aim of this book is to give you the tools to develop your own unique swing. Put them to work and you can start to build a reliable and powerful action. Human mechanics and the forces of nature make the swing happen. This information is easy to grasp. It's not secret or exclusive to a few insiders; it's simple and achievable.

How hard you work is up to you. Practice is the formula for success. Once the movement is ingrained in your long-term memory you can enjoy the game while navigating your way around the course.

Some players, particularly beginners, may need to check the basics, the nuts and bolts of the swing such as grip, posture and ball position. This information is fundamental to building a sound action and is in chapter 5.

CHAPTER 2

HOW TO BACKSWING

A confident start

I asked a friend who was having golf lessons, 'What part of the swing do you find the most difficult or annoying?' Without any hesitation he said, 'The backswing!' This is not unusual; just getting the body in motion can cause great anxiety. Some players stand over the ball for ages while they check their stance or worry about what to do with their shoulders, hips and knees. But too many swing thoughts cause confusion — and a shaky start puts the whole swing under unnecessary pressure.

The backswing should happen with little conscious thought. We are aiming to get to the point where taking the club away from the ball becomes an automatic routine. When you have less to think about, you have less to worry about and you can focus your attention on getting the ball to the target. During the backswing you need a clear head and a calm mind.

The backswing should be easy but millions of golfers are still puzzled by how to do it. We are told to 'take the club back low to the ground', 'keep the clubface square', 'turn the shoulders ninety degrees' and, for good measure, 'keep the club shaft on plane'. That kind of advice can be helpful but I found it wasn't very practical, especially when many of the top players regularly flout the conventions. For instance we are warned against lifting the club by breaking the wrists too early in the first stage of the takeaway. Yet many of the best players do exactly that — it was a signature of Seve Ballesteros' backswing.

The triangle mystery

Every year I'd head up to the newsroom to see the unedited vision coming in via satellite of practice day at the British Open. It was always informative to watch the contenders working on their swings — but one year I saw something that really caught my attention. This particular incident provided more evidence that we have made the backswing far too complicated.

Our cameraman was recording the players on the driving range. Among them was Seve Ballesteros who had already won the event three times. I watched with interest as he hit one good-looking shot with a fairway club. Fortunately, the camera kept rolling because on the next backswing he stopped abruptly when the club reached the top, and he held it up there. I was wondering what he was doing when into the frame stepped a swing coach who reached across and moved Seve's right elbow a tiny bit wider.

They were checking 'the triangle', a shape made by the forearms and an imaginary line running from elbow to elbow at the top of the backswing. When that line is parallel with the ground and the shaft is pointing along the target line, the backswing is deemed to be good.

Oh no, not the triangle! A successful backswing depends on how we use our hands. Wherever the hands go the arms have to follow and so does the orientation of the triangle.

However, many top golfers never get their arms set in the 'correct' triangles. Their elbows and clubs end up pointing every which way at the top of the backswing; some even drop the club down way past parallel. The best example is the big-swinging John Daly. At the end of his extreme wind-up, the club head almost touches his front leg. And if you drew a line across his elbows the base of the triangle would be tilted steeply towards the sky.

The hand—brain backswing guide

Consider the model of the homunculus in chapter 1 and the large amount of space the brain assigns to the hands. The link between your brain and your hands is so strong that the rest of your body has little choice but to react at all times to what your hands are doing. I began to understand that the movement of the hands must affect the quality of the swing. In fact, the backswing is governed by the hand—brain connection. Recognizing this basic aspect of human physiology makes the backswing a lot easier to comprehend and perform.

The first problem solved — your hands control the club on the backswing. It cannot move of its own accord.

My search for a reliable swing started to come together when I stumbled on some new clues from Ben Hogan. After he died in 1997, *Golf Digest* magazine published a tribute to Hogan that included quotes and photos collected over the years. When I read what he had to say about the backswing, it confirmed my suspicions about the significance of the hand–brain connection.

Roll your hands away from the ball

Hogan's first suggestion was to fan the clubface open at the very start of the takeaway. He said when training the movement he would 'roll the face open as fast and as far as I could'.

To fan the clubface open, you have to roll your hands away from the ball. This was an entirely different approach so I gave it a try. Instantly my backswing became an emphatic and fluid movement. All those worries about how to get the club in motion were gone. The effect on my confidence was astounding. Until now my focus had been on the club when it should have been obvious that it can't go anywhere *unless the hands lead the way*.

Watch the champions do it. During the first stage of their backswings nothing is moving apart from their hands and arms. As their hands travel further, the hands gradually draw their arms, shoulders, torso and hips around with them. The kinetic sequence is preordained, all guided by the hands.

It is important to understand that Hogan was not recommending a fast backswing; hasty starts can cause all kinds of problems. This was only a training technique he used to firmly establish the action in his long-term memory. In your own practice sessions, don't be apprehensive about taking the club away as smartly as Hogan suggested. It might seem drastic but it gives your hands a powerful way to ingrain the movement. Learn to trust your hands and they will guide you confidently through the backswing every time.

try this: Without a club in hand, put your palms together as though addressing the ball. Now move them across your body slowly as if making a backswing. Immediately they will begin turning over, with your left palm facing down and your right palm facing up. As this happens, the upper part of your right arm folds against the side of your chest and your elbow rests at your hip. This natural movement of your hands ensures a well-defined backswing pathway.

The dominant hands

Let your left hand and arm control the club

Hogan's second big backswing clue was that his left arm swung across his chest. He said, 'Poor players and even some tour players try to do it with the right arm. You have to do it with the left arm'.

Hogan's statement makes the point that during the backswing the *left hand and arm* are in control of the club. The right hand plays only a supporting role. It doesn't get fully into the action until it joins the left hand for the impact phase of the downswing.

As Hogan's hands rolled away from the ball, his upper right arm folded against his side. It was snug and tight throughout. Even on a full backswing, his upper right arm never moved far from his body.

try this: To feel how this backswing motion happens quite naturally, grip a club and take the address position. Begin the takeaway by rolling your hands and club away from the ball, over towards your back foot. The face of the club opens, your left arm stays close to your chest and your upper right arm folds neatly at your side. This anatomically correct outcome is caused solely by what you did with your hands. There is no need to force the movement; it should feel easy and composed. Allow your hands to find their way and the message about the power and influence of the hands will come in loud and clear.

Your hands lead and your body follows. Move your hands and arms away slowly and purposefully. As your upper body turns, your feet, legs and hips provide stability.

Hands, the brain and balance

The swing is a vigorous movement that involves your whole body and it is perceived by your brain as a threat to your balance. Your brain works with your finely tuned inner-ear balance mechanism to maintain equilibrium at all times. The word *equilibrium* comes from the Latin, *aequilibrium*: 'aequi' means equal and 'libra' means balance.

Poor balance is one of the main reasons that shots go astray. Whenever balance is compromised, your brain immediately starts to make adjustments. It will even override your intentions. Give your hands the freedom to coordinate and guide your backswing. Confident hands and a stable lower body will keep you inside the safety zone and out of danger.

Hands and balance. This is dynamic balance in action and it's no accident the hands are at the apex. At the top of a fully turned, well-executed backswing, a perpendicular line can be drawn from the hands through the hip and down to the ankle.

The backswing trigger

Most players use a personal body signal to get their swings started. Bobby Jones said his left side began the move. Jack Nicklaus swiveled his head to the right, away from the ball. Other players press their hands forward or kick a knee in towards the ball. The trigger helps to get the body in motion.

Ben Hogan put great value on his pre-swing 'waggle'. He made small hand movements for delicate shots and bigger ones for a full swing. The waggle was his clever technique of mentally rehearsing the whole swing.

However, the first signal to the brain that something big is about to happen comes microseconds before anything else. The last three fingers of the left hand tighten on the grip and the message flashes instantly from hand to brain — get ready, the human is about to move.

Your centre of gravity

Regardless of shape and size, all bodies have a centre of gravity. It's defined as the central point of the mass of the object. When you are standing upright, the spot is inside your body, slightly below your navel, roughly between your navel and your spine. When that central spot is supported, your body is in equilibrium and will not fall over. All of us have different body mass and height so it's useful to find your own centre of gravity.

try this: Because you have to lean your upper body forward slightly to address the ball, this simple test helps to establish and safeguard your centre of gravity. Grip the club in both hands then lean back onto your heels and forward onto your toes to gain a sense of your tipping point.

If you teeter off-line easily, try lowering your centre of gravity by concentrating on a spot in your abdomen region, just below your navel. It's much easier to stay in balance on both the backswing and the downswing if you maintain a low centre of gravity.

Finding your centre of gravity

The ugly reverse pivot

The dreaded reverse pivot

A reverse pivot is typically a beginner's mistake. It usually happens when your hands go *straight up* instead of moving the club around your body. If your hands go too far up and over, your body compensates for the unexpected shift in the centre of gravity by bending sideways at the waist. When your body is tipped over it's unbalanced and control is lost. A reverse pivot will work against your ability to make a sound backswing. It looks ugly and never delivers crisp ball contact. The ball can go anywhere and usually does.

The conventional backswing motion of the hands and arms is a *circular path* around the body. As the hands move they turn the upper body around the pivot point over the back leg. Lift the club vertically if you prefer but be careful to maintain your centre of gravity at all times.

Your hips play a major support role

Your hips are the link between your upper and lower body, and consequently they play a vital role in keeping your body stable so that it can turn and swing your arms. Your hips work in tandem with your feet and legs to brace your torso as backswing energy builds. On a full swing your hips have to work harder to keep the energy in check while playing their part in maintaining balance.

There's no need to intentionally manipulate your hips into any specific position. Your hips only respond to how far your hands travel. For a quick appreciation of what the hips do in the backswing, study any of the professionals. Their hands and arms are in control and their hips only turn back as far as required for the shot.

Slowly does it

Taking the club back without haste gives you control. Hurrying causes an abrupt off-balance action and a predictably dodgy outcome. The old saying, 'Finish the backswing', is really a hint about going back purposefully in a well-balanced flow all the way to the top.

One of my bad habits was rushing the backswing. I remember a sharp comment from the club professional as he watched me blow a shot: 'Hey, Steve, can you make that backswing any faster?' I got the message and began working on slowing it all down.

The professionals provide great examples of how to use the hands and arms slowly and deliberately. They take the club away gradually through a long, wide arc. As their hands reach the apex and backswing pressure reaches maximum load, the club's momentum causes their wrists to cock. When and where that happens in your backswing is dictated by the club you have in hand. Then everything waits until your feet are ready to fire. When ballet dancers or ice skaters are about to perform a big leap there's a quiet moment just before takeoff where they seem to 'collect themselves'. In that brief instant before the launch, they are calmly gathering the power of mind and body.

The only way to defeat a hasty backswing is to practice starting your takeaway ever so slowly. By making a deliberate backswing for every club, you are able to maintain equilibrium while ramping up the energy. And when the action is unhurried your brain can stay cool and unflustered. There is no need to rush — the ball isn't going anywhere until you hit it.

Martial arts like Aikido, Kung Fu and Karate are explosive rapid movements. But during training the emphasis is on simple actions that are done slowly until they are ingrained. The aim is to react without thought, without the brain getting in the way. The same philosophy can be applied to the golf swing.

The GRF, torque and backswing power

There are two powerful energy generators in the backswing: torque resistance and the GRF. The word *torque* comes from Latin and means 'to twist'. Torque is generated as your hands and arms twist your upper body around in the backswing. You can feel it building in your abdominal and back muscles,

try this: To appreciate the heaviness of your arms, make a backswing without a club and stop at the top for a moment. Then simply push off from your back foot and relax your arms at the same time. This creates an irresistible force that drops your arms and swings them down through the impact zone. Don't rush this test because it's about understanding the weight of your arms and the role of your feet in both ends of the swing.

Arm weight test

The sway. To prevent making this fundamental balance error, swing the club up and around your back leg — don't leave it outside your feet.

Golfers stuck on the shifting-weight model are prone to overload their right side in the backswing. This results in a pronounced sway to the outside of their back foot and an immediate threat to their balance. Then when they attempt to transfer weight by heaving their body back the other way, more often than not they get stranded back there. Every time I consciously tried to move weight to make the downswing, I found myself falling back away from the ball. The outcome was either a weak slap or a big slice. Forget about moving body weight because there is none to move. Get your feet moving so that your body can swing your heavy arms.

Shaping your own backswing

There are as many backswing styles as there are golfers; and your backswing can be as individual as you like. Trust your hands to lead the action. As the club moves back, the movement of your hands and arms alone will bring all the other parts into play.

Keep your hands low and play long

There are plenty of professional swings on the Internet that show that many players don't use a high hand action. Even on a full swing, their hands stop near but never way above their shoulders.

try this: Many players at the top levels of the game are capable of making a big turn of their upper body, with their hands finishing well up above their shoulders. This exercise tests your own backswing flexibility.

Grip the club normally then remove your top hand. Use only the hand that's lowest on the shaft (for most of us that will be the right hand) to lift the club up to where you consider is the top of your backswing. Then, without lowering the club, reach up with your left hand to see if your can complete the grip. If you find it a strain to get all the way up, you'll realize the tour players are much more supple than you. Don't copy their backswings unless you are capable of the high-hands, big power turn.

The backswing stretch

Go online and compare the hand action of legends Jack Nicklaus and Arnold Palmer with two of today's stars like Geoff Ogilvy and Matt Kuchar. All four players are champion ball strikers yet they have totally different backswing styles.

Nicklaus and Palmer both had lively upper and lower body actions. They made big hip and shoulder turns and took their hands up quite high. To accommodate their steeper backswings, their front heel came well off the ground. In contrast, Ogilvy and Kuchar don't take their hands up as far and their front foot stays planted.

While online, check out Allen Doyle whose backswing is easily the shortest ever seen on tour. He turned pro at age 46, won the Nike Tour three times and won the US Senior Open twice. He employs a wide stance and a truncated backswing where his hands barely rise above waist level. Yet he is able to hit more fairways than most.

Ben Hogan kept his hands relatively low and still gained tremendous energy in his backswing. In fact, his left hand and arm turned his upper body around so far, he said, that his chin stubble wore holes in his shirts near the end of his left shoulder.

Recent advances in club-head, shaft and ball technology also mean that you can achieve distance with less than a full backswing, which is good news for older players and the not so supple. When your swing is compact the middle of the fairway can be a lonely walk.

Should the left arm stay straight?

To hit the ball a long way, does your left arm have to stay straight to keep control of the club or can your left arm bend a little at the top? Some say it doesn't matter, others say it does. With so many excellent yet very different swings on display, the evidence agrees with both points of view. Younger, fitter golfers are capable of getting high compression into their grip and wrist with a straight left arm on a full turn. But if your arm needs to bend a little, let it — plenty of good players do.

According to biomechanical experts, more than thirty parts of the human body are involved in making a golf swing. For the body to work efficiently, flexibility is desirable, necessary and natural. The action is a dynamic athletic movement. Even the club shaft flexes quite markedly.

What about wrist cock?

A big deal is often made about wrist cock as some players need to know if their wrists are working properly in the backswing. However, the cocking or bending of your wrists is a natural reaction to the momentum of the club as it swings back.

During the backswing your wrists begin to break around waist height — whether they go earlier or later is not important. Let your hands lead, and work on using your legs and hips to brace your turning upper body. Your wrists will take care of themselves.

Wrist cock is a reaction to club-head momentum. It happens naturally so don't worry about it.

However, un-cocking your wrists too early on the downswing must be resisted at all costs. Throwing your arms at the ball from the top down, instead of driving with your legs from the ground up, causes weak shots.

Catching the backswing plane

There is a lot of discussion about the value of swing planes. But if you trawl through videos, books and the Internet, you will find plenty of disagreement about how many there are and where to find them. There's also debate about whether the plane is determined by the hands, arms, shaft or clubface. I like to think of the swing plane as the route established by the arms and club as they go back and forward.

Judging by the unorthodox actions of champions like Jim Furyk, Raymond Floyd and Lee Trevino, the backswing plane doesn't seem to matter much at all. The only plane of any consequence is the *downswing* plane, and those three golfers manage to find it every time.

Jim Furyk's wonderfully eccentric backswing proves the point that it's all about the downswing plane. He stands much closer to the ball than most players and, at the takeaway, his hands defy all the common conventions. He lifts the club vertically above his feet and well outside the centre of gravity.

But on the downswing he regroups and sets the club back where he wants it, on plane and inside the target line. To accommodate his close hand position, he releases his right side with a dramatic and early hip clearance. This unique style gives his arms and hands enough space to bring the club back down and swing it very effectively. Furyk's decisive legwork is the key factor that allows him to keep his downswing on plane.

try this: Here's a way to find the backswing plane that suits you. Begin by sweeping your hands out and away from your body in a wide arc. Then, in gradual stages, move the club through several backswing planes — high, low and levels in between. The point of the exercise is to find the backswing plane that fits your style and temperament. Above all, it should feel balanced, comfortable and easy to do. You can take the club back any way you want, but take care not to lose your centre of gravity on the way down.

The hands guide the way — the left arm is across the chest, the upper right arm is folded against the side. The backswing is stable, balanced and on plane.

Ben Hogan's backswing slot

Ben Hogan credited finding the plane of his backswing as his biggest breakthrough. He said 'it helped my whole swing, my whole game, my whole attitude' and gave him the confidence to become 'a golfer of true championship caliber'. He admitted his backswing never felt 'satisfactorily grooved' until he developed a method of getting on plane every time.

Through experimentation and diligent practice, Hogan found an easy way to take all the fuss and bother out of the backswing. He called finding the backswing plane 'hitting the slot'. He imagined a sheet of glass resting on his shoulders and worked on keeping his hands and arms below the glass, brushing the under surface with his left arm.

When studying videos of Hogan's swing, I noticed that after his hands and arms rolled away from the ball they worked close into his body and stayed there all the way to the top. By keeping his left arm across his chest, he was assured of making a repetitive movement. That's how he 'grooved' that solid, dependable backswing.

Compare Ben Hogan's backswing technique with that of Rory McIlroy, who does it very differently. During the first stage McIlroy moves his hands and club further away from his body. His backswing plane is much *steeper* and he doesn't get the club in behind until his hands are above waist level. His upper right arm separates and maintains the gap right up to the top.

Hogan's hands barely moved above his right shoulder, even when wielding a driver. Hogan and McIlroy prove it doesn't matter which route the club travels, as long it gets back down where it belongs for the critical part of the action.

Whether your hands move through a low backswing plane like Hogan's, or finish high above your shoulders, or somewhere in between, is up to you. Trust your hands and arms to find your own backswing plane.

Getting set

The carpenter's motto is 'Measure twice, cut once'. The same degree of care applies to the backswing. When taking the club away, the main factors are control and confidence. If your backswing feels comfortable and solid it's probably on the optimal plane. There's no need to rush; it should all happen smoothly. Some professional backswings might look faster than others but the difference is only marginal at best.

The vital part comes in the downswing phase. What really matters is making an on-plane and well-timed swing at the ball.

Through the first stage of the backswing, your hands and arms are the only body parts making obvious moves. While your hands and arms are doing the initial work, the rest of your body is quietly waiting its turn in the sequence.

As your hands go further around and up, your legs and hips share a bigger load. At the top, your hands and arms have turned your shoulders and torso into position. Now everything is set for the downswing.

CHAPTER 3

THE DOWNSWING DYNAMICS

The downswing sequence

So here you are at the top of the backswing. You generated strong ground reaction forces via your feet and legs and robust torque between your upper and lower body. You are all set and ready to go, so what comes next? How do you swing the club at maximum speed without losing balance or power on the way through? The answer lies with your feet and the earth beneath them.

Most suggestions for starting the downswing ignore the natural logic of the sequence. We are told to turn the hips, shift weight or pull down on the club. It was that kind of advice that had created so much confusion for me in my quest for a reliable swing. It focuses on *isolated links in the chain* instead of on the whole action. I found I was constantly getting stuck and my swing had no flow.

The best players produce club-head speed, distance and accuracy by using their feet and legs to exploit the GRF. Some employ a strong lower-body action while others are quieter. But, whatever the method, they all respect the correct sequence of the downswing — feet and legs first, hands and club last. Grasp this fundamental fact and you are well on your way to a good swing.

Your feet and legs hold the GRF and your upper body has generated plenty of torque. The downswing is ready to go.

The pressure moves from your back foot to your front foot and your right side begins to release. Your hips turn back to square and your arms drop into place with your upper right arm against your side. Your hands and wrists are still fully cocked. Your left arm begins to separate from your chest and goes back along the same route that it came from.

This shot captures the art of timing. Your right arm is still slightly bent. Your right hand is working with your left so both can swing the club through the bottom of the arc.

The transfer to the front side is complete. Your arms are straight, your head is down, your right side is relaxed and the ball is in flight.

When the energy is given free rein the result is a textbook finish.

Feet first in the downswing

Remember the model of the homunculus in chapter 1. While your brain allocates a lot of capacity to your hands, your feet get their fair share too. Your feet are critical for balance but they are also your only contact with the ground — and that's the big hint. The downswing unwinds from the ground up. The sequence begins as the pressure shifts from your back foot to your front foot. The momentum then travels rapidly up through your legs, hips and torso and out to your arms.

The old boxing maxim is 'Get the feet in first and then throw the punch'. It applies to any sport where your feet are in contact with the ground. Imagine trying to pitch a baseball without using your feet and legs. The throw would have no potency and the ball wouldn't get anywhere near the plate. Propelling a ball hard and fast demands a deliberate shift from your back foot to your front foot to release the GRF.

The same principle applies to golf. Staying on your back foot disrupts the transfer of energy and results in a weak swing. Without a decisive move to your front side, your upper body has no option but to fall away from the shot. The only chance of getting the club anywhere near the ball is to take a wild swipe and hope for the best. The common result is a big wide slice.

A typical error — staying on the back foot

The best players take the energy up a notch by moving onto their front foot just as their hands are reaching the end of the backswing. This early shift onto the front foot is like a mechanic's wrench putting a little more torque on a wheel nut. The hands, arms and upper body get an extra tweak. At that point the backswing is fully loaded.

Getting onto your front foot as fast as you can produces greater momentum and more club-head speed. I had seen Greg Norman's brilliant footwork in action during the event in Queensland. His dynamic shift to the front side produced tremendous thrust and club-head speed.

Shifting onto the front leg early in the downswing keeps the momentum going in the desired direction. The move brings the upper body back to where it started from and provides your arms, hands and club with the ideal line of attack. The club head will strike crisply.

To appreciate the role and influence of your feet in starting the downswing, take Sam Snead's advice and have a go at swinging the club in bare feet.

Lower-body technique in the downswing varies from one golfer to the next. Jack Nicklaus and Arnold Palmer drove hard with their feet and legs. Many of today's professionals also use a robust leg action but others keep their feet and legs fairly quiet. Whichever method you use, the priority is to maintain balance and control while doing it.

Kick in the right knee

A professional I played with a few times used to slap his thigh and say, 'just kick in the right knee'. That piece of advice would come after I had blown a shot. He always said it and I always ignored it, because he didn't explain it clearly and I didn't know what he meant. He just knew it worked for him.

Being told to 'kick in the knee' seemed too simplistic and disconnected from all the other bits I was trying to piece together. But I should have pressed him for more information because it was significant. The light-bulb moment came much later when I was studying downswing sequences frame by frame. *The knee has to break inwards*; it's a natural response to the back foot making the first move to release the GRF. It comes early in the downswing sequence and happens naturally.

Leave your hands till last

Many golfers can't figure out why their shots lack power. They swing hard at the ball and it flies straight enough — but doesn't go very far. A weak swing is commonly caused by a premature attack by the hands, also known as *casting*.

Letting go too soon. If your hands and arms are given free rein right from the top, it disrupts the correct sequence of the downswing and throws everything off plane and out of balance.

Going at the ball with your hands and arms from the top of the backswing causes your wrists to release too soon. If there's no decisive shift onto your front foot, your whole body is forced to hang back. The club head arrives at the ball ahead of your hands and the result is a swing that has no real vigor. To maximize the potential of the downswing, lead with your feet. It might seem counterintuitive to drive the downswing upwards, via your feet and legs to your torso, but remember it's your body that swings your arms, not the other way round.

The Golf Show's video library provided the opportunity to make frame-by-frame studies of amateurs and professionals as they made the transition from backswing to downswing. Close observation of the less skilled players provided striking evidence of the power and influence of the hand–brain connection.

If their hands stirred at the top of the backswing — even by the slightest amount — before their feet were engaged, the shot was in jeopardy. Their brain and body responded immediately to what their hands were doing. Their shoulders and torso rotated, their hands released their wrists too early and the energy fizzled out. You had to watch carefully but these tiny premature hand movements reset the balance mechanism and disrupted the order of the downswing.

Timing the hit

The New Oxford American Dictionary defines timing as the choice, judgment or control of when something should be done. As an example of the word in context it adds: 'One of the secrets of golf is good timing'. If the golf swing does have only one big secret, that's it — timing is everything.

Greg Norman compared timing to a race where everything arrives at the finish line together. To achieve good timing your whole body has to be coordinated and working harmoniously. You often hear a good swing described as 'being connected'.

The downswing plane

To make solid, and well-timed, contact with the ball, your arms, hands and club have to be on plane. The plane is the path that your club travels during the swing and that path is obviously determined by your hands and arms. As the upper body moves back above the ball, your left arm brings the club back down again. Both arms begin to rotate, staying on plane as they approach the ball to swing the club.

Arms on plane to deliver a well-timed swing. With your left arm across your chest and your upper right arm locked in place, you are now set to swing the club through the ball. Make no mistake; the position of your arms means the difference between making a good golf swing and a mediocre one.

The most effective path comes from inside the target line, down along the arc, through the ball and then back inside the line. Check your divots because they tell the story. Ideally a divot must start under and forward of the ball and show a line towards the target. If the line points too far left or right there's a good chance your downswing plane is faulty. Another way to check your own swing plane is to shoot a video of your swing.

try this: Here's an easy way to find your downswing plane. Make a backswing and hold the club at the top for a moment. To start the downswing, switch pressure from your back to front foot, let your right side go and instantly your hands and arms will drop into place. Hold this position — you will see that your left arm is across your chest; your upper right arm is sitting snugly at your side and your hips are to the front. Your hands have not released. You are now deemed to be in the power slot — the optimum position to work your hands and arms fully into the swing.

Repeat this exercise until you are familiar with this critical move because learning how to bring your arms and club down onto an efficient plane lies at the heart of building a reliable golf swing.

The secret to finding the most efficient downswing plane is the correct use of the passive dynamic transfer. Decisive footwork gives your hips a little push and your arms drop into place. To get onto the ideal plane, there's no need to consciously force the upper part of your right arm or elbow into your side. Done correctly it happens automatically.

The esteemed American teacher Harvey Penick called getting onto the downswing plane 'the magic move'. He believed it was 'weight shift' that brought the right arm and elbow back into the body. Ben Hogan said he got his arms onto the correct downswing plane when he turned his hips back to the left. Both Hogan and Penick knew that getting the arms and club back on plane, inside the target line, was the only way to achieve the best result. They just had different interpretations of how to get there.

The role of your right arm

Most golfers don't realize that as the club approaches the ball, their right arm should still be slightly bent. It does not straighten fully until just beyond impact. The action is similar to throwing a ball across your body, side-arm style. Acceleration is achieved by straightening your right arm at the right time. It reminds me of shutting a door — the hinge or pivot point is your right elbow. Grasp this fundamental point and you can start to develop decisive ball contact.

The role of your right hand

Whether you are right or left handed, the front side of your body leads the way in both the backswing and the downswing. Most people are right handed, so the right side of their body is more dominant. But an overly eager right hand is a swing killer for many players. If the natural tendency of your right hand is given free rein, it will begin to dictate the action too soon and will push the club across the target line and off plane.

Although your right hand's contribution is very significant, it should not be allowed to overpower your left — both hands must still work together. Train your right hand to wait while your left arm and hand guide the club back down on plane to the ball. Keep both hands relaxed or quiet and your brain will automatically tighten up your hands at impact.

Let it swing — releasing both hands

To achieve good timing, your hands must release at your wrists at the right moment so that the club can swing and accelerate through the ball. Search for high-definition pictures of professional downswings, because the last part goes by so fast it's difficult to see exactly when their hands release to time the swing.

Throughout the entire swing your hands describe a circle, but the club head itself travels along an oval-shaped curve. As your hands drop to waist level and begin to release your wrists, the club sweeps outward. It picks up pace at the widest part, through the bottom of the arc. After collecting the ball it travels back inside the target line and continues curving around your body.

Amateur golfers often have a wrong impression of the club's swing path. They try to square the clubface to the ball well before it approaches impact. Manipulating the route of the club is not necessary. Your hands, if allowed to work properly, swing the club head through an arc — it never travels in a straight line.

Picture perfect follow through — as the ball is struck, everything keeps turning around to the left: the clubface, hands, arms and body included. A dynamically executed full swing finishes fully over onto your front leg, with your hands above your shoulder and your body facing the target.

Energy release and club-head speed — the passive dynamic transfer

Until I appreciated the role of the passive dynamic transfer in the kinetic chain, it was always a struggle to swing the club at maximum speed. The passive dynamic transfer converts the energy generated during the backswing into an accelerated and well-timed downswing. Whether they realize it or not, all good players use this highly efficient technique to give their swings fluency and power.

Your feet set the passive dynamic transfer in motion. It begins when you move the pressure from your back foot to your front foot. Then your right knee breaks inward, your hips turn and your torso moves back above the ball. This sequence drives the energy up your body and out to your arms. However, the energy can only travel freely if your right side lets go. Any tension held in your hips and shoulders hinders the flow.

Load up and fire. Archery and golf are both target sports and they work on similar principles. The archer draws back the arrow to load the bow with energy. The golfer draws back the hands and arms to load the body with energy. The archer fires the arrow by simply letting go of the string. The golf swing works the same way — load up and let go.

try this: Make a backswing and hold the position. As you begin the downswing, forget about your hands and arms for a moment and rapidly shift the pressure from your back foot to your front foot. At the same time, let your right side go — don't leave anything behind. The momentum of your body and the weight of your arms will pull you through the shot and onto a well-balanced finish.

You can perform this exercise fast or slow. Either way it generates a quick acceleration of your arms and club. This is all about building awareness of the passive dynamic transfer and how it enables you to drive energy up through your body and out to your arms and hands.

When your hips and shoulders are relaxed, your arms can swing with total freedom. Passively held hips and shoulders allow your arms to move smoothly into the best position to time the hit and accelerate the club through the ball. You don't have to force any particular body part into position; it all happens naturally.

Timing and acceleration are essential elements of a powerful swing and both can be achieved by an efficient use of the passive dynamic transfer. Without timing, you won't get accuracy or distance; and you won't get either without acceleration.

Letting the energy out. Your right side has released and all the pressure is now over your front foot and leg. Your torso and head are still down over your bent right knee. Your hips and shoulders are quiet. There's ample room for your arms and hands to do their job, driving the momentum through the ball to the target.

Accelerate or perish

Newton's Second Law of Motion defines acceleration as the rate at which an object changes its velocity or speed. The formula is $F = Ma$, Force equals Mass times acceleration.

To apply force to the ball, the mass of the club head must be accelerating. And for the physics to work in timing the swing, the club head must be allowed to accelerate at the right moment. The club head reaches its highest velocity just beyond impact.

Centripetal force for speed and distance

The term *centripetal* comes from Latin and means 'seeking the centre'. The downswing is held together by centripetal force. The professionals put real zip into their shots by exploiting it to maximum advantage. They hold their hands in towards the centre during the downswing so that the club head can accelerate along the arc.

The same science is in play when a wheel is spinning: slow at the hub and fast out around the rim. The technique applies to all shots whether short or long.

This is the centripetal force at work. Your hands hold towards the centre, the club head accelerates along the arc of the swing.

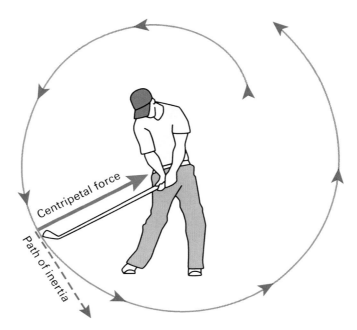

Pulling power. Centripetal force is explained by Sir Isaac Newton's Law of Inertia (also known as the First Law of Motion), which was published in 1687. The term *inertia* means the tendency to do nothing or remain unchanged. Newton's Law says that an object will remain at rest or will not change speed or direction unless acted upon by an external force.

Centripetal force also plays a big part in timing. To time the shot, the club head must be accelerating through impact. This is fundamental golf swing science. To achieve it effectively your hands must travel back to the same position where they came from at address. Centripetal force also contributes to good balance because it keeps the upper body stable. You can learn to promote centripetal force by keeping your hands inside the swing arc, holding them in towards your centre of gravity.

try this: This simple test shows you how to create club-head speed. Swing a club back and forth a few times. To start the downswing, wait for the pressure to shift from your back foot to your front foot. Then, as your right side lets go, hold your hands inwards towards your navel, your centre of gravity. Straightaway you will feel the weight of the club head and its potential velocity. There is no need to do this experiment forcefully. Merely tugging the grip moderately towards your body will make the club head feel light and fast.

MYTH   CENTRIFUGAL FORCE

Centrifugal force is a wrong-headed golfing notion that has gained prominence over the years. The term *centrifugal* comes from Latin and means 'fleeing from the centre'. Theorists believe this force pulls your arms and club away from you in the downswing. However, apart from a minuscule gravitational effect, there is no force dragging on your arms and club. The laws of physics established long ago that centrifugal force exists only in the imagination. The force that produces club-head speed is centripetal not centrifugal.

try this: To understand the actual forces involved in the downswing, attach a weight to a string and spin it around in a circle. If you let go, the weight will fly off at a tangent, along the line of inertia. It won't take off at a right angle, straight out from the centre 'centrifugally'. As the weight rotates, your hand directs the force inward not outward. The tension in the string is the centripetal force.

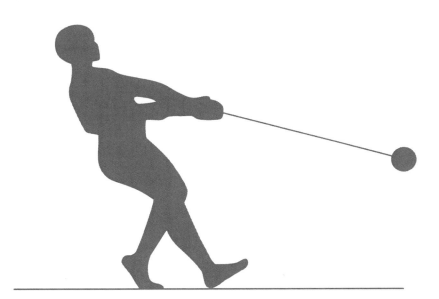

Athletes in the sport of hammer throw generate centripetal force through their hands, legs and feet. As they pull the hammer inwards it accelerates around their body. In the golf swing your hands, aided by your feet and legs, apply the same centripetal force.

Acceleration and the short game

If you want to chip or putt a golf ball, accelerate. Don't slow down. Acceleration through impact is essential for all ball sports. The best players accelerate their bat, racquet, hand or foot — whether they are 50 meters from their target or just ten.

Footballers who wrongly equate close with being gentle are almost guaranteed to miss shots on goal, often from point blank range. As they attempt to 'nurse' the shot, their foot decelerates, momentum dies and the ball deviates off-line. Soccer's penalty shot is a prime example. Players who get blocked by the goalkeeper are usually trying to be cute when they should be kicking with all-out conviction. Even snooker players can miss very short shots if the cue does not accelerate into the ball.

Deceleration is defined as speed slowing over time. It's a subtle sensation and difficult to detect; but, if the club slows as it approaches the ball, expect a poor result. Golfers are regularly hoodwinked by this phenomenon because they don't realize they are doing it, especially on short shots and putts. Deceleration often happens because the backswing is too big for the distance required. The brain detects the problem and, to compensate for the over-swing, the player unwittingly slows the club as it approaches the impact zone. The outcome is always second rate.

Kick with authority. Xabi Alonso of Spain, beautifully balanced over the ball, fires in a penalty shot against France in the Euro 2012 quarterfinals. He scored twice and both goals were perfect examples of timely acceleration.

Accelerate through the
chip shot.

If your short shots are going off-line or losing distance, try tightening up. Use a shorter backswing and go at the ball with deliberate accelerated force. Get onto your front foot and release your right side as quickly as possible. The result is a pitch or chip that's hit with authority. Professional golfers throwing up a high shot with a lob wedge might look as though they are swinging slowly; but you can be sure their club is accelerating through the bottom of the arc as it catches the ball.

try this: Here's a simple way to understand how to accelerate your short shots. Try hitting a few zingers, low-flying shots that come off a very abbreviated backswing. Take the club back to just around waist height, keep your right elbow tucked in, get your feet working smartly, release your right side and whip the club through the ball.

Beating the bunker

It is depressing to watch someone pile on the strokes as they attempt to get the ball out of a bunker. They stab at the sand, the club stays embedded and the ball barely moves. It's the only shot in golf where you don't actually hit the ball. To free the ball and beat the bunker, the club head has to accelerate under the ball to splash it out above a wave of sand. Pick a spot behind the ball, keep the face open and whip the club through the sand. Go at it aggressively and keep the club moving.

Under and through

Riding the sand wave

The fairway trap

Fairway bunkers

Strategically placed fairway sand traps are not the same as greenside bunkers. They require different tactics and skills. Because you are still a long way back from the green, to achieve distance, the clubface has to contact the ball before the sand.

You can promote better control and balance by gripping a little further down the club. Lean more towards your front foot and keep your lower body quiet. Don't be too cautious — take to the shot vigorously. If your lie is good and there's little or no lip to block the shot, have a go with a fairway club. Swing confidently, keep the club head accelerating and remember to collect the ball first.

Putting

There's an old golf expression, 'Never up, never in'. A lot of players don't give themselves a chance. Their putts fall short of the hole more often than they roll past it.

Whether it's a short tap-in or a monster roll, give the ball a good confident rap. An accelerating putter head generates pace and, with pace, comes your best chance of the ball falling into the cup. One of the best putters of all time, Ben Crenshaw, said 'the pace of the putt ... is more important than the line. Pace is vital'.

Keep your head steady, let your eyes follow the ball.

Successful putting demands a rock-steady head because it's all about balance and control. If your head shifts on the forward part of the stroke, your body will change its alignment. Even a slight head movement can take your arms and the putter on a slightly different route than the one you intended.

While watching the closing holes of a major professional tournament, I saw one of the world's most experienced players constantly missing short putts. His lead was evaporating. The TV commentators were blaming his arm action while failing to see the real cause of the problem. The player was losing confidence and he was taking a nervous little peek on the forward part of his stroke. As his head turned to look at the hole it came up just enough to pull his arms, shoulders and putter away from the target line.

During a full swing it is almost impossible to hold your head in place. However, if a player's head moves while putting, even on short putts, the ball is likely to miss the hole most of the time. The best putters make a fluid accelerated stroke and they don't look up until the ball is long gone. Take aim, keep your head still and putt smoothly. When practicing, don't spend all your time sinking long putts. Ignore short putts at your peril — they can kill you in competition.

Rhythm not muscles

According to legendary golf instructor Ernest Jones, a golfer achieves distance through 'effortless power, not powerful effort'. Jack Nicklaus said if he needed to hit the ball long he always made a point of starting down slowly. That way he could control the swing while maintaining balance, rhythm and timing.

The term *rhythm* is derived from Latin and Greek and means 'to flow'. One of the best ways to understand golf rhythm is to imagine a car on a gravel road. If you step on the pedal too hard and fast, the wheels spin as they try to find traction and the car fishtails all over the place. The same principle applies to the golf swing. Don't ruin all the preparation by going at it fast from the top down.

Many years ago two elderly women golfers gave me an eloquent lesson in rhythm and timing. On the first tee it was obvious my opponents were not long hitters. While their shots landed down the middle, they didn't go very far. Here was my chance to demonstrate some power golf.

Unfortunately, my out-of-control swing meant my second shots often required miracle recoveries from deep rough or adjacent fairways. My opponents, meanwhile, were chatting and walking together down the middle. Mercifully they didn't gloat too much — apart from a few mocking comments like 'How was it over there?' and 'We never go that far on our holidays'. Needless to say they beat me senseless.

The lesson: there's no need to muscle the swing. You are using a lightly weighted golf club to launch a small white ball; it's not a sledgehammer for breaking rocks. Find your balance and rhythm, take off smoothly and then bring on the power.

Australia's Karrie Webb uses rhythm to great advantage. She makes a long, slow backswing that sets up perfectly for a well-balanced and accelerated swing. The skill of launching a golf ball long and accurately comes from knowing how to let the energy out in an organized way. The golf swing is not about going flat out with the throttle open at all times. It's easy to get ahead of yourself through an eagerness to go hard at the ball. But golfers who rush into the downswing are prone to get well out of sync. Though the ball might fly a fair distance it is usually off-line and heading for trouble.

If you have a tendency to bolt and mistime the downswing, try making a very slow backswing. It's easier to time the shot if the first stage of the downswing is under calm management. A steady pace promotes good rhythm and is the best way to overcome a hasty downswing. For a demonstration of two truly rhythmical swings, look for Tom Purtzer or Steve Elkington on the Internet.

Fred Astaire's swing tempo

The Russian ballet star Rudolf Nureyev nominated Fred Astaire as the greatest dancer of them all. Nureyev might have guessed that Astaire was also pretty handy with a golf club. Dancers and golfers at the top of their game share the same qualities: balance, rhythm and timing.

I saw Astaire showing off his golfing prowess in a 1938 movie called *Carefree*. It was set in a country club and he played the part of a psychiatrist, Doctor Tony Flagg (golf pun intended), who tried to impress the girl (Ginger Rogers) with his golfing skills.

In a dazzling trick-shot routine he hit several balls with a short iron before picking up a fairway club to fire a string of shots way down the range. Filmed from behind, the balls are seen soaring into the distance. He managed to contact all the balls cleanly while dancing and pirouetting nonstop. Unfortunately for Doctor Flagg, the girl went home early and missed the show.

Astaire didn't need brute force to get distance. He made the golf swing look easy because his brilliant footwork delivered rhythm and timing. And as the old song says: 'It don't mean a thing, if it ain't got that swing'.

CHAPTER 4

CLUES FROM THE MASTER – BEN HOGAN'S SWING

The Hogan mystique

Ben Hogan's golf swing was a compact and highly efficient action. It was a style unrivalled in his heyday and few have been able to match it since. Jack Nicklaus named him the best ball striker bar none. Those privileged to hear it said when Hogan connected with the ball it sounded like a gunshot. No wonder it's the swing many golfers still look to for inspiration.

Hogan had an impressive playing record, made even more remarkable by his comeback after a crippling car crash. He worked tirelessly to understand the mechanics of the swing and practiced longer and more meticulously than his peers. He was motivated by the belief that it was possible to birdie every hole. He admitted he never achieved perfection but said he came pretty close at times.

In competition Hogan was all business. He was out there to win tournaments, not friends. After teeing off, his mind was solely on the game and he hardly ever spoke to fellow competitors. Some say he was cantankerous and aloof but others remember him as friendly and generous. Whatever the truth about the personality behind the name, Ben Hogan will always be one of golf's immortals.

A last look, Ben Hogan, 1985

In 1948 alone, the year before his car accident, Hogan won 10 tournaments. His playing future looked assured until the horrific head-on with a Greyhound bus changed everything. He fractured his collarbone, ribs, pelvis and ankle. Doctors said he might never walk again let alone play golf. But barely two months after being admitted to hospital, the 36-year-old defied the odds, went home to recuperate, and began working on his swing. Nine months later he came second in the 1950 Los Angeles Open.

Resigned to hobbling around on damaged legs, Hogan won another three US Opens, the Masters twice and the British Open in 1953. When the conquering hero returned from his famous Open victory in Carnoustie, Scotland, thousands turned out to cheer him in a ticker-tape parade through New York City.

Did Hogan have a secret?

According to folklore Hogan did something out of the ordinary that guaranteed he could make a superb swing every time. There are many theories. Some believe it was a twisting action he made with his left elbow before starting the backswing. Others think it had something to do with the extra spikes fitted to his golf shoes. The speculation is endless.

Another line of inquiry focuses on a hand technique he said allowed him 'to cup his left wrist'. 'Cupping' refers to the left hand bowing slightly inwards at the top of the backswing. It was apparently his way of defeating a troublesome hook that had developed earlier in his game.

Whether this feature of the hands is important, or just peculiar to Hogan, is still open to debate. If you study the backswing hand and wrist positions of professional players, you'll see a great variety. Some wrists cup just like Hogan's, others are flat and in line with the forearm, while some bend noticeably the other way. It doesn't seem to matter much. The most important hand position happens at impact.

One of Hogan's best 'secrets' is not a secret at all. It comes at the start of his classic book, *Five Lessons: The Modern Fundamentals of Golf*. The first sentence of chapter 1 says, 'Good golf begins with a good grip'. The quality of his grip meant more to him than just his connection with the club. Playing the Open in bracing Scottish weather, he carried a hand-warmer in each pocket because he said cold hands affected the feel of his whole swing.

The fascination with Ben Hogan's swing is an obsession with many golfing enthusiasts. If you need proof of his near spiritual status go online and search 'Hogan's swing' or 'Hogan's secret'. You'll find millions of links to forums, blogs, books and opinion pieces. Anything he wrote or said is scanned for hidden meaning; videos and photos are scrutinized frame by frame. Every conceivable single aspect of his swing is dissected and analyzed in the hope of discovering Hogan's 'secret move'.

Despite his books, interviews and the visual record, the skeptics are not convinced Hogan told the whole story. They reckon he solved the mystery and didn't share it. But how much can one man conceal when his swing was and still is on constant public display? Whenever he was asked if there was a secret he gave vague and cryptic replies. He once famously said that the secret was 'in the dirt', a not so subtle hint that maybe we should get the clubs out and do some of our own digging.

What is evident from all viewpoints is that there is no quick fix. Learning is what humans do best and we never stop doing it. Think about your golf swing as a work in progress — Ben Hogan did.

The big clues

When Hogan died at the age of 84 in 1997, *Golf Digest* magazine published a tribute with the headline 'The Last Look He Gave Us'. It included quotes from his books and interviews and several photos. Hogan's condensed swing advice was exceptional enough but the pictures of him swinging a four iron when he was 72 years old really caught my eye.

The pictures were taken twelve years earlier in 1985, to coincide with the *Golf Digest* edition of *Five Lessons: The Modern Fundamentals of Golf.* The magazine reported that 'In the process and to our astonishment, Hogan agreed to pose for new color photographs ...'. For the now almost reclusive Hogan to have his swing recorded was very surprising indeed. He was still practicing every day but usually away from prying eyes.

Photographer Jim Moriarty was assigned 'the intimidating task of capturing the great man's swing on film' — and it all happened in just one 45-minute session. Moriarty reported: 'He hit four irons and from what I could tell he hit them well'. But Hogan, ever the perfectionist, was less than satisfied. He apparently cursed after every shot and could not be persuaded to use the driver.

One of his eyes was apparently defective and he was having trouble seeing the ball. He said, 'In order to hit the ball flush, I have to feel that I'm going to top it. I've got no depth perception'. Despite his very poor vision that final look at his swing was a timely reminder of Ben Hogan's style and power.

Photo of Ben Hogan taken at the session with Jim Moriarty in 1985. Hogan is just into the downswing and perfectly balanced over the ball. His hands and arms have the club on plane and ready to go. He's in the prime position to guide the club back down for a decisive swing through the ball. You can almost feel the energy he is about to unleash.

The power of the hands

The quotes included in the *Golf Digest* tribute were fascinating. Hogan's straight-to-the-point swing advice really stirred my interest. Some of these tips were new to me and I was immediately absorbed by every word.

One of Hogan's quotes was about starting the backswing. He said, 'Training myself, I would roll the face open as fast and as far as I could'. Hogan's surprising but straightforward statement validated my growing awareness of the significance of the hand–brain connection. To roll the clubface open, you have to roll your hands away from the ball. At last, here was a practical and worry-free way to make a backswing. The *hands* lead the backswing — everything else follows their lead.

Look at any video footage or sequential photographs of Hogan's swing. As soon as his hands roll away from the ball, the clubface opens and his arms work close in to his body. As the motion continues, his arms, hips, shoulders and torso are drawn into a superlative backswing position. His feet and legs are the platform holding the backswing in place. Nothing else needed attention — his body posture set the stage and his hands conducted the orchestra.

The left arm guides the swing

The *Golf Digest* edition of Hogan's book included a new foreword by Nick Seitz, the magazine's Editor in Chief. It was based on an interview with the great man, and it offered a new and vital swing clue.

According to Hogan, 'Most people are too upright because they disconnect the arms from the body. My left arm swung right across my chest on the backswing, and was the strongest part of my downswing. It's almost impossible to get your body out of position and come back to the ball badly'.

This emphatic comment about the left arm came nearly thirty years after his book was first published. Many seem to have missed this critical information. I can only guess most readers skipped the foreword and started at chapter 1.

Connected and on plane

Hogan's deceptively simple left arm technique kept him connected and the club on plane every time. At the start of his backswing, his hands fanned the clubface open, his left arm swung across his chest and his upper right arm folded very early. Even on a full swing his upper right arm barely separated from his torso. It remained snug and tight through the backswing and stayed connected as the downswing began. He discovered the method through painstaking research and it served him very well.

This photo from the 1985 session shows Ben Hogan in the middle of the downswing with his left arm and club shaft perfectly on plane. His lower body moved first, shifting onto his front foot and leg. His left arm is guiding the way, pulling his right arm into position for his hands to release and swing the club head through the impact zone. His right arm will not straighten fully until it's past the ball.

It's obvious that Hogan's left hand and arm govern the motion as they guide the path of the club in the backswing. However, as he said to Nick Seitz, he also believed his left arm was the strongest part of his downswing. How his left arm brought the club back down on plane is a vital part of the action and deserves closer attention. The downswing starts with the action of the lower body but the left arm guides the movement of the club.

Watching Hogan swing

The man himself can be found on the Internet giving a masterly swing demonstration. The video clip runs just over a minute but contains everything in one neat package. In the preamble he only talks about the downswing because, as he says, it's the most important part. Fortunately, we get to see his whole swing in slow motion.

There are many ways to make sense of the action but if you had to define an orthodox swing, Ben Hogan's would fit the bill. Watch closely.

Feet and legs for ground control

During the video demonstration, watch Hogan's feet and legs and you will understand how the GRF intensified during his long, sweeping backswing. Hogan's right foot was a rock. When he set it in place he was ready to start. It was his anchor point for loading the GRF. It didn't move again until he started the downswing. Hogan built tremendous energy as he turned his arms and body over his back leg — it was a strong pivot point. And if he had extra spikes on his shoes, maybe their job was obvious.

Study the slow motion video of Hogan closely and you'll see that just as his arms and club neared the top of the backswing his feet initiated his lower body's change of direction. He never actually stopped moving. The momentum was merely held in check for a brief moment. As he shifted rapidly onto his front foot, his hips squared up again and his torso moved back to the ball to bring his arms into position for the hit.

As Hogan drove his feet and legs in the downswing, his torso, head, shoulders and hips were quiet. His lower body did all the initial release work. The momentum moved over onto his left leg and his right side let go. This allowed his left arm to bring the club down onto the most effective plane, time and time again.

The backswing stabilizers are your back foot and leg and your hips. The easiest way to make a backswing is to allow your hands and arms to turn around your back leg.

Hogan had his own strong view on how he started the downswing. He said quite emphatically, 'the hips initiate the downswing'. But he may have been fractionally ahead of himself. The hips are slaves to the feet and legs. They can't work effectively by themselves.

> try this: Here's an experiment that proves how unproductive your hips are without the support of your feet and legs. Lift your back foot off the ground and then turn your hips as if to make a downswing. The result is a weak and awkward movement. For your hips to work properly they need your feet and legs fully engaged with the ground.

Although Hogan said he cued his downswing to his hip turn, be careful of turning your hips too fast, as this action can spin your torso around prematurely. This error throws your shoulders and arms outwards, leaving the club no alternative but to cut across the outside of the ball instead of attacking it from inside the target line. Hogan was well aware of the upper body's tendency to rotate early. He warned against it when he said the downswing 'starts down below with your knees and your hips'. And, remember, just before your knees comes your feet.

Timing is everything

Hogan developed an awesome swing because he knew the secret of good timing. As Hogan's hands reached waist level, his left arm was across his chest, the upper part of his right arm was securely against his side, elbow at the hip, and his hands were still fully cocked. He held that pre-fire position until he could no longer resist the gathering momentum. The video clearly shows that his hands and wrists maintained the same angle formed during the backswing all the way down *until he released them* to swing the club.

During Hogan's downswing, the only parts of his body that moved at speed were his hands and arms — they alone applied accelerated force through the ball via the club. As Hogan approached the impact zone his hands seemed to slow down a little. He kept the grip end of the club in towards his body, stayed connected and exploited centripetal force to maximum effect.

Hit the ball hard with both hands

Hogan was a recognized power hitter. He said his left hand kept control of the club but he wished he had three right hands so he could apply even more power to the shot.

The video of Hogan's swing demonstrates his superb technique. As he drove onto the front foot and whipped the club head through, all his concentration was on hitting the ball as hard as possible. He didn't hold back. He wasn't afraid of taking a divot either — on iron shots his hands really dug the ball out. Maybe that's what he meant when he said the secret was 'in the dirt'.

Hand position at impact

Hogan put a lot of emphasis on the correct movement of the hands. He was adamant that as the club head made contact with the ball, the back of the left wrist should be facing the target. This seems obvious because the leading hand has to be facing the target to square the clubface and collect the ball accurately. But as Hogan pointed out, many golfers tend to do the opposite without being aware of it. Their weak lower bodywork leaves the face of the club open at impact and delivers an inferior shot every time.

Thinking about hitting the ball with the back of the left hand helped my swing tremendously. It produced crisper ball contact and the momentum carried me easily to a full finish.

Welcome to the show

In an appearance on *The Ed Sullivan Show* in 1953 Hogan gave an exhibition of how to swing the club easily — it was the same tip he wrote about in *Five Lessons: The Modern Fundamentals of Golf.* At address he recommended tucking both elbows in towards your hips, and to think of your upper arms as being joined to the side of your chest, not just connected at your shoulders.

Using only his feet and legs to drive the motion, he swung the club back and forth at half pace a few times. He then began to lengthen the arc and power up to a full-throated swing.

Hogan's TV appearance clearly shows how your legs drive the momentum up through your torso, out to your arms and hands, and finally to the club. If the downswing respects the correct sequence there's no need to resist the urge to use your hands. You can let them loose at the very moment they're needed. It's worth the effort to find the complete segment, if only to see Hogan's comic send-up of Ed Sullivan's swing.

Hard work wins every time

Hogan once remarked, 'I don't think God had golf in mind when he made us'. He knew the swing was an unnatural movement that had to be developed. He cited Sam Snead's elegant swing as an example saying, 'It didn't come naturally. Sam had to practice it just as anyone does'.

The power and momentum of Hogan's swinging arms and club carried him into a beautifully balanced follow-through. Note how he's on the left leg, facing the target with his hands now over his left shoulder.

Hogan admitted his early career was going nowhere until endless toil on the range gave him the results he needed to play at the top level. He said if the other players worked on their game for two hours a day he worked eight and would happily have done twelve. He told a television interviewer that 'over and above winning tournaments' it was practice that he enjoyed most of all. He loved working on his game because it gave him 'great satisfaction each and every day'.

Smart practice and a tireless work ethic are the only ways to develop a reliable golf swing, or anything else for that matter. Talent alone is not enough. People become champions in their chosen field because they devote extra time to their weaknesses and persist until problems are solved. Take Ben Hogan's sage advice and keep at it until the swing gets firmly lodged in your long-term memory. Practice — smart practice — is the only realistic way to find a reliable, repeatable swing.

CHAPTER 5

FIRST AID FOR YOUR SWING

NUTS AND BOLTS

If professional players feel their swings need work, they always check the basics first. When your swing feels like a stranger and nothing seems to work, go back to first principles such as grip, body posture and ball position.

Posture at address

The quality of your posture at address affects your whole swing. You should feel comfortable and balanced at all times. If your posture is sound your muscles won't fight one another. It's easier on your body, especially your back.

At address stand fairly tall, bend slightly at the waist and lower your whole body to the ball via your knees. This ensures that your hips remain above your ankles (your points of support) and preserves your centre of gravity.

A relaxed posture promotes freedom of movement. So stand tall and give your arms plenty of room to swing the club efficiently. Avoid stooping, leaning your head and shoulders too far forward, because it blocks your ability to make a free turn. Practicing the chin-up and butt-out posture might look and feel strange at first but you will soon settle on a body position that feels comfortable.

A well-balanced stance at address means that your hips are positioned above your ankles so that your centre of gravity is protected. Keep your chin up, stick your butt out and maintain an almost flat line from the top of your spine to your tailbone. Holding your head up helps your upper body turn more easily.

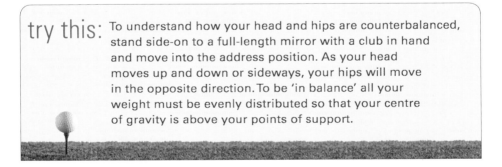

try this: To understand how your head and hips are counterbalanced, stand side-on to a full-length mirror with a club in hand and move into the address position. As your head moves up and down or sideways, your hips will move in the opposite direction. To be 'in balance' all your weight must be evenly distributed so that your centre of gravity is above your points of support.

All good swings are ruled by how well the golfer maintains balance. Balance is always king. Height and body mass vary and your centre of gravity depends on your shape and size. It is easier to stay in balance if you lower your centre of gravity. Establish your tipping point by leaning back onto your heels and forward onto your toes.

Both illustrations are examples of poor posture and bad balance — lordosis on the left and kyphosis on the right. *Lordosis* means an inward arching of the spine in the lower part of the back. *Kyphosis*, where shoulders and spine are hunched over, is equally bad.

Front-side bias

A lot of the older books of instruction promoted a front-side bias, especially for iron shots. Tommy Armour recommended setting up slightly towards the front foot for all clubs except the driver. He wrote about it back in 1954 in his book, *How to Play Your Best Golf All The Time.*

Ben Hogan noticed that some of his fellow professionals would 'list their bodies' towards the target as they took their stance. Hogan also put a little more pressure on his front foot and leg at address. It's illustrated quite clearly in *Five Lessons: The Modern Fundamentals of Golf* and it's plain to see in photos and videos of his swing.

Hogan's method was to turn his front foot out towards the target while setting his back foot at a right angle to the target line. He looks as though he's aiming his whole body into the shot. He said this attitude gave him a better line of attack because his front foot was already pointing in the direction he wanted the ball to go.

A front-side bias can remedy a consistent slice. Leaning towards the target at address might help players who fall away from the shot as they swing down. A front-side bias makes it easier to get onto the front leg early, which ensures a more efficient swing path.

Towards the front foot at address

The grip

How you grip the club affects the whole action. Bring both hands together with the little finger of your right hand either interlocking or overlapping your left hand's index finger. The main thing is to fit your hands together as closely as possible so that they can work as a unit.

Both hands on comfortably

The only part of the grip that seems to have any bearing on control and security are the last three fingers of your left hand. When primates evolved to a point where they could hold a stick firmly with these three fingers, the combination of hand, arm and stick made a very powerful weapon. It's not called a club for nothing.

The strength of the left hand grip varies widely from player to player. Firm or light — it's up to you.

For power and control, left-hand grip pressure is primarily in the last three fingers.

try this: Experiment with your own grip pressure. Start by gripping the club firmly with the bottom three fingers and then apply the others as lightly as possible — just so it won't fly out of your hands. Try swinging with drivers or long irons. You'll probably be amazed at how far and how accurately you can hit the ball with a super light grip. It works because it's virtually impossible to have tension in your body when your hands are soft. This test encourages a swing that's smooth and relaxed with a lively release through impact. Try it out on the practice range as a way to develop greater freedom and better acceleration through the ball.

Ball position

The arc of your swing determines your optimal ball position. At address there are two ball positions in play. One is the location of the ball between your feet and the other is the distance between you and the ball.

The ball between your feet is roughly the same spot for all clubs — about the middle of your stance or a little forward of that spot. As the clubs get shorter, the width of your stance narrows and starts to open up, meaning your front foot turns out and your hips and body aim more towards the target, almost facing it for chip or pitch shots. If your stance is too wide for the short clubs, your hip turn and follow through will be restricted and the shot predictably weak.

The distance between you and the ball defines an efficient swing path. The ball should always be easy to get at. The two main faults are over-reaching (stretching your arms out too far) and cramping-up (not leaving enough space for your arms to work freely). Both affect balance, accuracy and power.

Look at down-the-line photos of professionals in the address position and you'll see huge variations. Some have their hands very close to their body while others prefer a longer reach.

If you're not collecting the ball cleanly, try setting up further back. Too close and you might be getting in your own way, blocking your hands and arms from making an effective downswing. You must be able to fully extend your arms through the impact zone. To achieve a truly athletic movement your arms need an unrestricted pathway, so take the time to find out what works best for you.

The standard ball position for the driver

Find the comfort zone
between you and the ball.

try this: To find your ideal distance from the ball, swing the club
back and forth a few times. Where the head brushes
the ground is approximately the lowest point in your
downswing. Now adjust your setup to find the ball
position that gives you a good clean swing.

Alignment

Aiming well away from where we want the ball to go is a common error caused
by stepping into position badly. One way to find the correct alignment is to
select a spot on the ground between the ball and the target, usually about a
club length or so in front of the ball. It might be a stick, a shadow or a patch
of dry grass, anything that does the job. But, remember, it's against the rules to
deliberately place a marker.

Move into position from directly behind the ball. Align the clubface and
set yourself parallel to the imaginary line that runs from the ball, through
the intermediate mark and on to the target. Don't just blaze away at the
wide-open fairway — aim at something. If your ball lands in a poor position
after a good swing, the problem could well be faulty alignment.

Seeing the correct line

Professional golfers never take their alignment for granted. On the practice ground they will place clubs along their heels or toes, like railroad tracks running to the target, or have someone stand behind them to check if their aim is good.

Divots

Many years ago, at my very first golf lesson, the teaching professional asked to see a few practice swings. After a while he said, 'Do you take divots?' Not appreciating the reason for the question I replied, a little too eagerly, 'No, I don't'.

'Well that's the problem, you are trying to lift the ball into the air.' He explained how the ball is struck a descending blow. The loft of the clubface propels the ball upwards; it doesn't need to be helped into the air. The divot indicates that the club head was still moving through the bottom of the arc as the ball launched off the face of the club.

On *The Golf Show* we recorded divots being taken in close-up slow motion. A viewer reported that the demonstration of the downward strike and resulting divot changed his perception of the swing. For years he had been trying to assist the ball into the air with a kind of scooping action. An early wrist break, especially on wedge and bunker shots, usually means the bottom edge of the club will strike the ball in the mid section. A skulled ball is never an ideal outcome.

But divots are not compulsory. The ball can be nipped off the surface cleanly — it all depends on the arc of your swing and the lie of the ball.

Building your own swing

Playing outdoors, in all kinds of weather, is a rigorous test of our physical and mental abilities. That's why golf is the most challenging game of all. When every shot demands attention, the last thing you need is an untrustworthy swing.

Balance is one of the biggest factors. It's easy to fall out of your intended swing arc when you turn your body vigorously and swing your arms. A **low centre of gravity** keeps everything stable. Take the time to find your body's tipping point. Develop your awareness of how the movement of your hands affects your balance and how your feet and legs work together to ensure stability.

Use your understanding of the **hand–brain connection** to simplify the backswing. Work on the conversation between your brain and your hands and feet until you can feel the forces that drive the **kinetic chain** reaction. Practice the movement by swinging a club backward and forward around your body until the action is ingrained in your long-term memory.

Ramp up the potential energy of your swing by exploiting the **GRF**. Your back foot and leg, along with your hips, hold the major load of the backswing. The downswing begins as the pressure shifts from your back foot to your front foot. When you move to the front side, the **pressure shift** between your feet releases the kinetic energy developed during the backswing.

The **passive dynamic transfer** is a vital part of the ground-up release technique. As soon as the pressure moves onto your front foot and leg, let your right side go. This decisive move brings your upper body back to the ball with your hands and arms in position to make an accelerated swing. Take advantage of **centripetal force** to keep your downswing stable and dynamic.

Work on your **rhythm and timing** until you are able to swing with confidence and time your hit. Small adjustments can lead to big or unexpected changes so go slowly until the movement is locked into your long-term memory. **Practice** the action until you have a swing that will stand up under pressure. When you know your own swing intimately the fun can really begin. Enjoy the walk.

AUTHOR ONLINE!

For more resources, visit Steve's website
www.thegolfswingexposed.com

INDEX

FEB 2014

CPSIA information can be obtained
at www.ICGtesting.com
Printed in the USA
LVXC01n0907141213
365261LV00025B/92

9 780987 341600